A Woman's Guide to Success and Happiness

HANDBOOK OF DAILY THOUGHTS AND WEEKLY MEDITATIONS

JON GONZALES
Hairdresser Career Development Systems

A Woman's Guide to Success and Happiness
Hairdresser Career Development Systems
Copyright © 2019 by Jon Gonzales

All rights reserved. No part of this publication may be reproduced, distributed, or transmitted in any form or by any means, including photocopying, recording, or other electronic or mechanical methods, without the prior written permission of the publisher or author, except in the case of brief quotations embodied in critical reviews and certain other noncommercial uses permitted by copyright law.

Although every precaution has been taken to verify the accuracy of the information contained herein, the author and publisher assume no responsibility for any errors or omissions. No liability is assumed for damages that may result from the use of information contained within.

Library of Congress Control Number: *2019914766*
ISBN-13:   *ePub:*   *978-1-950073-75-7*
          Hardcover: *978-1-950073-68-9*

Printed in the United States of America

GoToPublish LLC
1-888-337-1724
www.gotopublish.com
info@gotopublish.com

A Woman's Guide to Success and Happiness

HANDBOOK OF DAILY THOUGHTS AND WEEKLY MEDITATIONS

JON GONZALES
Hairdresser Career Development Systems

SECTION 1

52 Thoughts on Success and Happiness

Here is a list of 52 important concepts for success and happiness, one for each week in the year.

Read them through, then go back and think very deeply about each one for an entire week.

See what new insights you discover as you think more and more deeply about simple ideas.

Excellence begins within

1 You'd better believe in yourself, because you're all that you've got.

2 Take charge of your life by overcoming the fear of failure with confidence.

3 Excellence begins within.

4 You control your own destiny. Unleash the power within.

5 Live up to your own expectations, not the expectations of others.

6 When you feel overwhelmed or stressed out, your body is telling you to take a break.

7 It's OK to be selfish once in a while. Find a little time for yourself.

8 Find a hobby or cause that makes you fulfilled and happy. Perhaps turn it into a home business.

9 It's okay to make mistakes; learn from them and move on.

10   *Develop a competitive spirit within so you can compete in the arena of life.*

11   *Excellence begins with a positive attitude. If you always look for the good in life, you will avoid negativity.*

12   *Procrastination is the thief of success. Never postpone important endeavors.*

13   *Always seek self-improvement.*

Seek Self-improvement

14 The door to education is never closed. The more you learn, the more you'll build self-confidence within yourself.

15 The happiness of your life depends on the quality of your thoughts.

16 Once in a while do something out of the ordinary by pampering yourself.

17   Stop worrying over things you have no control over.

18   When you get a little down on yourself or are having a tough day, always remember other people may have bigger problems than you.

19   Be thankful for the gifts of life such as family and good health.

20   Too busy to be happy? Then you are too busy to enjoy life.

21   Stop worrying about tomorrow, live life to the fullest each day. Today is all we have.

22   Challenge yourself every day to improve on yesterday.

23   If you don't develop a passion and desire for self-improvement, you will be setting the stage for mediocrity in your life.

24   We are all creatures of habit; make sure you form positive habits about your growth and development.

25   Use the words "I can" every day instead of "I can't."

26   Confront and overcome fear of failure with determination.

Persevere

27 Dare to meet the challenges of life head on.

28 Don't be afraid to fail — failure is just part of the learning process. Learn from your mistakes and move on.

29 Persevere! Never give up. You only fail when you fail to get up.

30 Take great pride in your appearance. When you look good, you feel good about yourself. This is a prerequisite to building self-esteem and self-confidence.

Laugh a lo

31 Dare to Dream. Anything is possible if you believe.

32 You're special. Tell yourself every day that you are special, because you ARE!

33 Eat sensibly and cut down on sugar and fatty foods. Eat fruits and vegetables instead.

34 Change your eating habits and you'll look and feel better. When you nourish your body, you'll have more energy.

35. Let it out — it's okay to let it out to cry and scream once in a while.

36. Challenge yourself every day to improve on yesterday.

37. Develop your public speaking skills. You will see a dramatic improvement in building self-confidence and it will widen your opportunities in the work force.

38. Prioritize and finish what you start. You will gain a great sense of accomplishment.

39. Read self-help books to help you develop powerful positive mental attitudes. Only think positive thoughts. Always look for the good in people and in life.

40. Take deep breaths and do some stretching exercises when you feel stressed.

41. Laugh a lot, and smile.

42. Hug somebody every day.

43. Visualize positive thoughts, like a Hawaii vacation, your children, grandchildren, the people you love.

44 Ride a bike.

45 Take a break or a bubble bath, listen to soothing music.

46 Treat yourself once in a while; you're worth it. Buy a new dress, get a facial, new hairdo or a massage.

47 Observe the warning signs of depression or burnout. Your body's telling you to take a break.

48 Gain a spiritual awakening with a little prayer, or meditation.

Ride a bike

49   Take the initiative in building friendships.

50   Never be dependent on any man for your financial security. You never know when you might have to go it alone. Invest in YOUR self-esteem and in making a good living.

51   Smile often, develop a dynamic personality, be a joy to be around.

52   Learn about money and money management. Read and follow Suze Orman.

Section 2

How to Find Your Winning Look

Jon's bonus feature on how to communicate with your hairdresser to get the right look for you.

Whether you want to look professional, build self-esteem, gain self-confidence or just want to feel good about yourself, your hair is your crowning glory.

You can wear expensive clothing, fabulous jewelry and accessories, but if your hair doesn't look good, a poor hair style will detract from your overall appearance.

Follow these tips with an open mind. A clear dialogue between you and your hairdresser will turn your salon visit into a truly special experience.

Find a top salon and hairdresser. *Get referrals from friends, neighbors or business associates. Even if you're shopping and see a great look, compliment the lady and then ask where she got her fantastic look. She will appreciate your compliment. Another way is to visit a few salons in your community, and ask if they give free image consultations.*

Communicate clearly with your stylist. *A clear dialogue between client and hairdresser is essential in finding a look that is uniquely just right for you. Lack of communication between client and hairdresser is one of the leading causes of customer dissatisfaction. You may not be accustomed to stylists who actually listen and truly care about exceeding your high expectations.*

Be patient

Keep your expectations realistic and practical. *What may look good on someone else may not be suitable to your unique facial features or hair structure.*

Keep an open mind. *Always keep an open mind to the suggestion of your stylist, listen to their opinions then offer your opinion. Make sure both agree on a style.*

Go for easy maintenance. *In today's fast-paced world, many men and women need easy to maintain hairstyles between salon visits. If you desire easy maintenance, let your hairdresser know.*

Be patient. *Perhaps your hairdresser will have to correct a poor haircut or poor style selection acquired elsewhere. It may require two or three visits.*

Feel free

Bring a Picture. *When visiting your stylist for the first time, bring a picture of a hair style for reference. Although the style may not be appropriate for you and your unique features, it'll help give your stylist some guidelines to better understand your beauty needs.*

Are you partial to long hair? *'A little off the top' can have many interpretations between you and your hairdresser. If you are partial to long hair, let your stylist know.*

Help your salon get better. *Top salons encourage feedback from their customers, good or bad. If you're unhappy, let the owner know. Help them improve.*

Feel free. *Most top salons encourage customers to feel free to select or change hairstylists within the salon. Never feel embarrassed or intimidated when you want to try another hairstylist in the salon. Most top rated salons want you to feel comfortable with any member of their team if your regular stylist is booked up or unavailable. Your complete satisfaction is all that matters, not their egos.*

Ease into change. *Never make a drastic change in a hairstyle, especially when going from long to short. Find your new look gradually.*

Adapt to change. Many people are unhappy with a new look simply because it's unfamiliar. Many feel they got a bad haircut. Give yourself time to get used to your new look… chances are you will be pleased. Change is always difficult, so if you're unsure about wanting a new look, make sure change is what you want.

Go for it!

Section 3

Powerful Prescriptions for Looking and Feeling Your Best

A guide to finding out how to look your very best.

A positive image will help you meet the challenges of business and life with confidence.

You and only you control your own destiny.

Beauty starts within. Beauty on the outside really means nothing if you don't feel it within.

Enjoy the moment

A great hairstyle and look will be a very inexpensive investment in feeling good about you.

Don't try to please everybody, please yourself first. Accept who you are by feeling good about yourself. There is no speed limit in finding happiness within. Life is short, enjoy the moment.

Clearly define happiness

Unleash the power within by maximizing your full potential. Dare to compete in the arena of life.

Read something positive 15 minutes before you go to bed.

Clearly define what will make you happy, personally, professionally, and financially.

Compassion and acceptance go hand in hand.

Get out of your comfort zone, be more assertive, dare to take calculated risks.

Eliminate feelings of inadequacy and intimidation.

Life is always worthwhile to the person who can laugh, love, and be happy.

Take full responsibility for your own success and happiness.

Don't let your appearance undermine your positive impact on others. You never get a second chance to form a positive first impression.

Don't allow yourself to be vulnerable by putting blind trust in relationships.

Begin today on a program of self-renewal and behavior modification.

Clearly define and measure your own strengths and weaknesses with an open mind.

Sometimes we place too much trust in others to make us happy.

Break the super-woman habit of trying to please everyone but yourself.

Unleash and develop the power within.

When you respond to yourself with compassion, rather than anger, guilt, or disappointment, you will be accepting yourself as the imperfect person you are. Learn from your mistakes and move on. It's okay to fail once in a while.

Overcome the fear of failure and rejection with confidence.

Happiness comes when we stop complaining about our troubles and begin to be thankful for the troubles we don't have.

Confront fear, anxiety, stress, and worry with confidence.

Life is either what you make of it or what it makes of you.

Always try to be a little kinder than necessary.

If you don't learn from your mistakes, there's no sense in making them.

Learn from yesterday... live for today... hope for tomorrow.

Positive thinking is the only way to produce positive results.

Success is not an accident, it's hard-earned.

The secret of success could be learning at an early age that you are not perfect.

It's lonely at the top, but you do eat better.

If you believe you have no chance to succeed, you are probably right.

The road to success is always under construction.

They say that education is expensive, try ignorance. To successfully combat gossip, ignore it.

Failure is merely the opportunity to start over again, wiser than before.

Think positively

Most failures come from people who have the habit of making excuses.

Knowledge is power, only when it is turned on.

The hardest part of climbing the ladder of success is getting through the crowd at the bottom.

Follow Jon!

For FREE weekly blogs, business tips, success tips, ongoing special events and a website filled with valuable information you won't find anywhere else, visit Jon's Weekly Blog:

hcds4you.com/blog/

facebook.com/jonhcds4you

twitter.com/hcds4youcom/

linkedin.com/in/jongonzales

Linkedin Group
linkedin.com/groups/4330607/

youtube.com/user/hcds4you

hcds4you@gmail.com
Toll Free: (800) 390-4237
hcds4you.com

About
Jon Gonzales

Jon's career spans over 43 years as an owner/hairdresser, seminar leader, business consultant, educator, motivational speaker, and author. He is a graduate of the University of Hard Knocks.

His no-nonsense down-to-earth educational programs and seminars for hairdressers, salon owners, teachers, nail techs, estheticians—and everyone involved in the beauty profession—are receiving rave reviews. They are imaginative, easy to understand and cost-effective. His programs are widely acclaimed throughout the United States and Canada for helping his colleagues reach higher levels of excellence.

Education is his only business.
Excellence is his standard.

Jon shares his proven real-world insights that can only be taught by a fellow salon owner and hairdresser who clearly understands the business and educational needs of his colleagues.

Jon is committed to making Hairdresser Career Development Systems a truly educational company you can trust and count on, free of any special interest groups.

Jon is committed to helping his colleagues reform education, raise their standard of living and improve the quality of their lives for themselves and their families.

Whether you're just starting a business or have years of experience, these tips will save you time and money, and serve as a roadmap in growing a successful and profitable business.

www.ingramcontent.com/pod-product-compliance
Lightning Source LLC
LaVergne TN
LVHW070436080526
838202LV00034B/2655